Zen
in the
Art *of* Golf

Joseph McLaughlin

This book is dedicated to every golfer who has
struggled and suffered loss:

*Know that you will be reborn again and that
peace and joy are yours at last.*

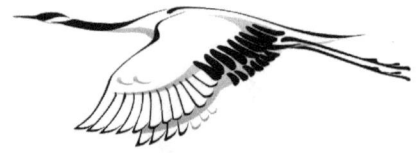

ZEN GOLF

All these things
are one thing

The white ball at rest
the silver face of the club
the green brush of the turf
as the shot is swept away

turn of the body
swing of the arms
leap of the divot
the click we seldom hear
as the ball is struck

the high, airy flight
against the sky
curving across the blue dome
as if on a string
connected
to the player's heart

It is not over
until the ball settles
softly on the ground
motionless again

All these things
are one thing.

–JM

Acknowledgement:

A special thanks to my daughter-in-law, Joan McLaughlin, for help in preparing this edition.

Third Edition 2019

Cover Photo: "Long Carries"
by Joseph McLaughlin, Myrtle Beach, 2006

ISBN 0914720090

Pale Horse Press
Dover, Ohio 44622

Table of Contents

BOGEY GOLF

Back in the late 1950's or early '60's, the USGA imported and promoted an interesting concept from England: *bogey golf*. The idea was that most golfers have a difficult time shooting par and that a bogey for a hole was a more realistic goal. Eighteen bogeys on a regulation course usually works out to a score ranging from 88 to 90 strokes. Golfers could then try to make a few pars and—with luck—an occasional birdie for a respectable mid-80's score and feel they had accomplished something. Some clubs even had score cards printed with the new-fangled "bogey" par for each hole.

When this was tried out by the management of our large municipal course, the gamblers scoffed. Even our irascible pro,

"Hooley" Zerby, a lantern-jawed West Virginian who looked absolutely Scottish in his Tam O'Shanter, spat on the ground when he heard the idea. "That's for amatoors," he declared to the gang in the cane chairs on the clubhouse porch.

In the end, the golfing Mafia and Hooley were right; the bogey golf idea lasted no longer than a slightly later experiment with leaving the pin in the cup for no penalty while putting. Each died about a year after birth in the USA.

But bogey golf is still a good idea for many of us. When I'm having one of those days, and nothing is going right, I immediately take the pressure off my game and switch to bogey golf. Instead of struggling futilely to break 80, I work at breaking 90 by comparing my score to level 5's (18 x 5 = 90). Note that you can pick up two strokes by parring a short par 3, and even a bogey 4 helps the cause. While this seems to be admitting defeat, any score in the 80's is better for one's self-esteem than one in the 90's! Playing bogey golf–level 5's–is my way of dealing with a bad day, and I have a few of those every season.

A variation of bogey golf is to mark up a score card with one's personal par for a course. For most of us, that won't be 72! Holes over 400 yards long can be played as par fives. Par three holes over 175 or 180 yards, I play as short par fours. Very long par fives, especially those over 500 yards, might be par six for some of us. Before a round, go through the card and re-mark it for yourself, retaining the regulation figure on the easier, shorter holes. When you add it up, your personal par for a course might be 81, 85, or even 90 strokes. This is a far more realistic goal than "par" for a course.

Now, have an average day, make a few "birdies" (pars), and you'll feel a real satisfaction with your round of golf. You might even end up five or six strokes *under* your personal par, and your achievement will be as valid as that 67 shot by the touring pro.

BREATHE!

"Count to ten when you're mad!" our parents and teachers always told us. As children we would ridicule this advice and count rapidly to ten before throwing our temper tantrums, as if to prove the advice didn't work, or to use it as a license for bad behavior. After all, we'd counted to ten. It wasn't *our* fault if it didn't work. Right?

Given the pace of living in the twentieth century, it's no wonder we can't take the time to even count to ten slowly. In fact, the ancient advice, now corrupted by our culture, is to *count ten breaths*. In/out–slowly– is "one". In/out again is "two". And so on until you reach ten. I guarantee you'll have calmed down by then. If not, begin again. Count to one hundred breaths if need be. By then the source of your anger will have melted away.

Nothing is more relaxing or refreshing on the golf course than to take a long, deep breath before each shot. Start by letting the belly out. As your lungs fill, let the shoulders rise. Then exhale long and slow. I like to hold a club horizontally with my hands spread apart on the shaft. Raise the club over your head as you inhale; then bend deeply from the waist, letting the club lead you down into a deep exhalation, as if you were doing a toe touch. (Warning: keep the knees bent while doing this.) Most people will think you're working on stretching your back muscles—not a bad idea either—and will never realize that you're energizing yourself with oxygen!

Much has been made in recent years of tennis players who "grunt" as they hit the ball. Some golfers have tried this with varying success. The idea is that exhaling on the swing through lets the athlete completely release the racquet or club, resulting in a more powerful stroke. In his wonderful book, *Quantum Golf*, Kjell Enhager teaches a similar process, advising the golfer "when you take the club back you must inhale, and when you swing—exhale...if you inhale and exhale in an easy manner, then you can swing a golf club in the same effortless manner." (Enhager, 43)

Unfortunately, Enhager goes on to complicate this idea by having the golfer say the words "super" on the backswing and "fluid" on the downswing. Even if one does this silently, it is *psychologically* difficult to "say" a word while inhaling. I find I cannot do both. I must either focus on breathing or saying the words. (Tim Gallwey, in *The Inner Game of Golf*, uses the words "back" and "hit".) For me the words work best. I do my deep breathing as I approach the shot, even telling myself out loud, "relax and make a good swing/stroke." Once I've breathed deeply and relaxed, I settle over the ball and thereafter breathe shallowly.

In fact, I want to forget about breathing at that point. One is reminded of the famous pro who was stopped along the fairway (in the days when the galleries could get close to the players) and asked, "when do you breathe during the golf swing?" Being a congenial fellow, the pro tried to observe his breathing in order to answer the question–and began mishitting every shot! The question became a mental trap which ruined the golfer's concentration. And many a gambler has successfully used suggestions of this type against his opponents!

Seriously, breathing can open doors to our inner lives. In meditation practice, breathing is the way to the "center" where the mind is quiet. In his book, *Peace is Every Step*, the Buddhist monk Thich Nhat Hanh describes his beautifully simple technique (p. 10) by advising us to "recite these four lines silently as we breathe in and out...

> Breathing in, I calm my body.
> Breathing out, I smile.
> Dwelling in the present moment,
> I know it is a wonderful moment."

Don't we golfers want to have calm bodies, smile, find our quiet centers, and dwell in the present tense? Sometimes under pressure we literally forget to breathe; the doors to our calm centers close and we begin to feel panic. This is quite natural when we are out of touch with ourselves. Worse comes to worse and manifests itself in anger and—later—regret.

Eventually, we'll recover, perhaps when the round is over, and the game is lost. We'll sigh deeply while changing our spikes or sipping a cool drink while adding up the card. At last we are relaxed–perhaps even depressed. The trick is to learn to relax our minds and bodies on the course, during the match–by *breathing*.

SOURCES

Enhager, Kjell. *Quantum Golf*, Warner Books. New York: 1991.

Gallwey, Timothy W. *The Inner Game of Golf*, Random House, New York: 1981.

Hanh, Thich Nhat. *Peace is Every Step, Bantam Books*. New York: 1991.

EGO

Last week, after getting my golf game off to an unusually good start, I found my concentration broken when I discovered I was even par through the fifth hole. I was so elated my conscious mind began planning how I'd describe my successful round to my friends and relatives. I began picturing the setting and rehearsing the words! "An even par round today," I'd crow.

The inevitable happened. I double-bogeyed the next hole and worked my way through the next twelve in another six strokes over par for a round of 80, close to my 9-handicap. I haven't played par golf on a regulation course for 30 years! Yet, there I was, more concerned with the opinion of others than quietly concentrating on the game at hand. This is a function of the ego.

As golfers we tend to believe we are better than we are. When the course or conditions prove otherwise, we immediately react by believing we are worse than we are, and this may work against us. Obviously, we need to monitor our self-talk. We need to be quiet, inside and out. We need to ignore the ego until it stops its constant chatter; vocalizing the ego's messages only gives it more power.

In his book, *The Inner Game of Golf*, Tim Gallwey has labeled the conscious mind (ego) Self 1, and the sub-conscious mind Self 2. Gallwey contends that Self 1 will always interfere with Self 2, given the opportunity. "In fact, Self 1 not only gave Self 2 instructions, but criticized him for past errors, warned him of probable future ones, and harangued him when he made a mistake." (Gallwey, 19).

PGA tour player David Ogrin agrees. "The subconscious does not make mistakes. The conscious does. The sub will make a perfect swing every time; the conscious can't or won't." (Ogrin, 47) Thus we tend to get in our own way as the ego orders us to try harder while focusing on scores we can brag about. What will we tell our companions at the office Monday morning? Worse, yet, here they are playing with us, after listening to all our golfing stories, and everything is going wrong!

Sometimes, in desperation, we cheat or lie. Nothing serious, just not counting strokes for a lost ball, teeing it up in the rough, knocking the ball out from under a tree. Again, these moments are products of the ego which is so concerned with outer appearances, material success, and reputations. In coercing us at these times, the ego interferes a great deal with our enjoyment of golf.

I call this part of my being "Joey." He is the person constantly trying to worry, distract, alarm, and instruct me. He is bristling with parental messages, negative commands, and distress. He can spin a nightmare of terror out of a nasty look or a harsh word from someone.

Imagine "Joey's" impact on my golf game. Hit the ball into a bunker or face a short putt and he begins his admonitions. Any success I have would put Joey out of work, so sometimes he even cheers against me. "Miss it!" he'll hiss when I approach a three-footer or a drive off the first tee with everyone watching. Even though Joey is most concerned with reputation and appearances, he really prefers being a victim.

Naturally, I don't want to surrender control to this resident genius. But the ego has an unfair advantage: In what other sport does one have so long to wait—and worry—before playing the next move? It is this constant anxiety about the future, nurtured by the ego, that does us in.

The necessity of dealing with the ego makes golf an ideal arena in which to practice meditation, which can be extended from quiet moments through all our activities. At first, one may need to begin by sitting quietly. A comfortable armchair in a pleasant room. No tv, no radio. Close your eyes and become aware of your breathing. Follow it until it becomes relaxed and steady. Listen to the "noise" in your head. Don't try to stop it. Just observe. Let those thoughts come and go. They are mere static on the surface of your mind. When they return again—and they will—merely note their presence and release them. Then return to awareness of your breathing.

Finding that deeper, calmer self through sitting meditation will enable us to contact it again during action on the golf course. We need to sit, observe, and release thoughts until it becomes natural to do so. Our ability to do this enables us to play our strokes unaffected by the ego. (Of course, we want to continue to use intelligence, another aspect of the mind. We need to be able to measure yardage, select clubs, plan strategy. But that is the subject of another essay.)

We've all played a few holes at a time in what the touring pros call "the zone." Our concentration is perfect. Nothing can affect us. The game is simple. Oriental philosophy calls that state "the void", even satori, enlightenment. What usually breaks our concentration, dropping us out of the void and back into a fully conscious state, is something simple. A peek at the scorecard, or a missed putt which we perceive as the beginning of the end. Fear and consciousness return, the blue jay of the ego lands shrieking on our heads, and our games return to their former levels.

All of this is perfectly natural. Our task is to learn to enter the void at will and to remain in it for longer and longer periods, during which we permit our calmer, deeper selves to become absorbed in the game. This is also a time when we can become unified with our bodies by "feeling" a good swing rather than thinking about fundamentals and individual movements of joints.

SOURCES

Gallwey, Timothy W. *The Inner Game of Golf*, Random House, New York: 1981.

Ogrin, David. "What's Your Personal Par?" *Golf Digest*, September 1987, pg 45-47.

GETTING IT GOING

"The idea of Zen is to catch life as it flows."
                                        --D.T. Suzuki

I caught the flow experience again. It appeared on the first hole of Sunday's tournament when I rolled in a 21-foot birdie putt. I felt very smooth and true and connected with the target as I watched the ball track toward the cup. It was one of the best strokes I'd ever made, and I still recall the exquisite feeling of hitting the ball so squarely, so perfectly. I could feel it rolling directly out of my heart.

This experience gave me a feeling of confidence that my *skills were equal to the task* as Stephen Wilson points out in his description of the flow state. Wilson discusses the work of Dr. Mihalyi Csikszentmihalyi which suggests that: "...flow occurs when a person's resources or skills are evenly matched with the demands of the activity in which they are engaged. When the requirements or expectations of the situation are greater than our capabilities, we feel tension; when we are over-skilled, we experience boredom or apathy. Flow spontaneously occurs when resources and demands are balanced." (Wilson, 22)

Golfers are always hoping to "get it going." Instinctively, they know that one good shot can turn the game around and save the day. (Conversely, one bad shot can ruin the day if not properly managed. Old golfers know that disaster lurks just beyond every tee and green.) Skills and good performance seem to ebb and flow, emerging spontaneously, staying for a brief time, then disappearing inexplicably. This phenomenon is at once the most enticing, then frustrating aspect of the game which keeps luring us back with siren songs then dashes our hopes just when we expect victory.

Csikszentmihalyi's research suggests we can do some things to initiate the flow state and perhaps retain it longer. Wilson says we need to alter our beliefs about the situations we face in such a way that we feel neither overly challenged or bored. This takes some work, however!

One thing that has helped me feel "equal to the task" is to set a personal par—which may be higher than the card—for a difficult hole. (See "Bogey Golf".) On the day mentioned above, I went on to the 442-yard second hole, intending to play it as a short par five. With the pressure off, I hit a short drive into the light rough on the right side, then a 230-yard 5-wood onto the green. (I never hit this club that far!) I two-putted for a "birdie" four and further reinforced my flow state. This happened on two more of the longest and most difficult holes that day. I felt completely confident and capable, yet very calm. I was immersed in the experience and found myself very much in the present tense, doing what I was doing, not looking forward nor back. I didn't let anyone tell me my score, and I was not mentally engaged in computing it. This delightful sensation enabled me to play the front nine in even par—with a few more fabulous putts—and lasted until the four-teenth hole.

There, I hit the tee shot on this long par three into a greenside bunker. I fluffed the ball out of the sand and just made the green. A normally satisfactory uphill 60-

footer stopped three feet past the cup. OK so far. Then I missed the little putt coming back for the only double bogey of the day, and I clearly felt the flow state begin to fade. An ordinary mortal then, I played the last four holes plus three for my 36-41-77.

Why couldn't I have sustained the flow state for the entire round? Where does it come from? Where does it go? Did the missed short putt unplug my connection so to speak? Did I begin to try to force the ball into the cup with some intellectual effort? Suzuki also has said: "The fact of flowing must under no circumstances be arrested or meddled with, for the moment your hands are dipped into it, its transparency is disturbed..." (Figler, 337)

Often, when a golfer believes he is over-matched by a shot, he'll miss it, shouting "I knew I was going to do that," as the ball bounds into the lake or trees. On the other hand, we can find boredom on the golf course, which also weakens our performance and negates the flow state. How often do we bogey the easiest, shortest holes on the course, believing we should have automatic birdies on these?

Wilson suggests that "being able to shift out of stress or boredom requires moving into the present moment and the realm of feeling." (Wilson, 25) Instead of being anxious about carrying the water hazard. shift your attention to stimuli such as the feel of the rubber grip in your hand, the feel of the grass as you brush the clubhead away from the ball, the pause at the top of your swing. Of course, you're not deliberately doing these things; you're merely going along in a state of awareness. (Reading the last few words and mentally rehearsing this for yourself, you found yourself in the present moment, didn't you? All thoughts of the water hazard were gone.) Now the ball is on its way, probably safely home since you slipped away from the stress and anxiety built into the shot—which might have made you feel unequal to the task.

As for those "easy" holes, can you find a new, more interesting way to play them, so you won't be bored? Perhaps you can hit an iron off the tee to have a longer second shot. Maybe you should deliberately hit the ball with a draw or fade to make the hole more interesting (but not too difficult!). One of the prominent sports psychologists suggested this to a tour player who was bored with the game. (Coop, 29)

Every player has entered the flow state accidentally. Check your scorecards and you'll notice strings of pars—and perhaps strings of bogeys and double-bogeys reflecting what I call a "negative" flow state. This occurs when everything is going wrong and seemingly everything you do only makes the situation—and the score—worse. As in my description of the double-bogey above, there seems to be an inevitability at work. Each mistake leads to another. First, I hit the ball into the trap. Then I hit a poor bunker shot. Then I three-putted. I couldn't stop it from happening.

Negative flow is just as hard to stop as positive flow is to initiate. While discussing this with a colleague, I hit upon the idea that flow is really a sine wave curving above and below a base-line, creating positive and negative cycles. "A master could reduce the negative side almost to nothing," my friend suggested. And isn't that what happens at the highest level of golf? A really good player would have needed no more than bogey four in my situation above.

When I interviewed Steve Anderson, our 1990 Ohio Amateur champion, we discussed a string of bogeys he made on the back nine which very nearly cost him the title. "I knew

I just needed one good shot to turn it around,"
Anderson said. He finally got an iron close to
the pin on a par three and finished strongly,
taking the championship in a two-hole playoff.
But I also noticed that while he was in a negative flow state, he salvaged bogeys rather than
making things worse by chipping and putting
quickly out of a sense of disgust. You could
almost see him nurturing his little pool of
confidence until it began to "flow" again and
become brimfull.

Wilson uses the term "balance" to describe the ideal conditions for flow to exist.
Certainly, the gifted young amateur golfer
was akin to a tightrope walker who falters
momentarily, flailing his arms, but finally
retains his balance--and his "flow."

SOURCES

Coop, Richard H. "Concentration", *Golf Illustrated*. August 1990, pp. 28-36.

Figler, Howard. *The Complete Job-Search Hand-
book*. Holt: New York, 1988.

Wilson, Stephen R. "Hatha Yoga and the Flow
Experience," *Yoga Journal*. Nov/Dec. 1992, pp. 22, 24-26.

GOLF CARTS

"The gemme is meant for walkin'."
  –Shivas Irons
  Golf in the Kingdom by Michael Murphy

"Panzers..." someone said, and we all turned and looked back at the tee from the fairway. Two occupied golf carts were sitting there, waiting. Then we heard the roar of another fleet coming down the tenth fairway. In the distance, others were circling the tenth tee. After the rain had cleared everyone from the crowded course, we thought we'd have the back nine to ourselves.

But it was not to be. In the first wave were some tenacious women who hit the ball frequently–and with some competence–then doggedly pursued their shots by flooring the gas pedals. We noticed all this as they played through.

"Those are our husbands behind us," one said as–in almost a single motion–she stepped from the still rolling cart with a club in hand, punched the ball 125 yards down the fairway, and remounted. "They'll probably push you, too," she added as she roared off after her pink ball.

We had been having a close and enjoyable match, taking our time on each shot without being unusually slow. As a foursome, we'd walked the front nine in two hours and ten minutes, and that included some struggles with rain suits and umbrellas.

The husbands overtook us as we putted out on the eleventh green. It was evident we were going to be expected to give way, and we accepted our fate, standing to the side of twelve tee until the spouses could get there. I watched them closely. Once all were on the green, one man held the flag about six inches above the cup while the other two putted simultaneously. Both missed, but the flag bearer kicked and swatted their balls back toward them while he replaced the stick. All had putted in less than 15 seconds! (All had missed, too.)

They jumped into their carts and raced for the tee where we were waiting. My playing partners politely stood aside, but I had to make a point. "We'll let you go through," I said. "But it doesn't seem fair that you all putt at the same time just to get the hole over with. There's no way we can keep our places on the course when you do that."

After a moment of embarrassed silence, one of the men growled, "Well, those guys behind us are pressing pretty hard, too." They hit quickly, not even taking practice swings, and set off after their women much as Rommel's WWII armored corps must have raced to escort German convoys across the African desert. By now, the roaring was all around us as two more sets of carts were backed up on eleven while the women went chugging by us on the next fairway. We were encircled by the enemy: golf carts.

Apparently, a man (or woman) in a golf cart is playing a different game. He becomes so intent on the speed of his play that he's willing (perhaps relieved?) to pick up his ball on the green without ever sinking it in the cup. A couple of salutary slaps toward the pin and it's on to the next tee. Are these people keeping score? Will haste be our salvation?

(One notes that—having said all the above—the introduction of motorized carts into the game has not had the effect of speeding play. Two public courses near me now require that carts be rented until 1 p.m. on the weekends. Other courses in resort areas do not permit walking at all. Yet I notice both have the starters timing people, and one of the public courses is threatening to send people off the course who do not complete a round in a specified time!)

In Michael Murphy's wonderful novel, *Golf in the Kingdom*, the heroic Scottish professional, Shivas Irons, talks to his pupil about walking the course.

"I notice ye hardly pay attention to the walkin' part.'

I admitted that I didn't. The next shot usually preoccupied me.

'Well, that's too bad,' he said as he looked into the fire, 'not many people do. 'Tis a shame, 'tis a rotten shame, for if ye can enjoy the walkin', ye can probably enjoy the other times in yer life when ye're in between. And that's most of the time, wouldn't ye say?" (Murphy, 178)

In between shots. In between work days. Rain showers. Wives. Tournaments. Jobs. Weekends. Meals. Irons is right: being "in between" is very uncomfortable in a culture where every minute, nay second, is valued as a commodity. So we transfer our rushing onto the course. The carts get us from shot to shot ever sooner, so we spend less time in between.

When I was first introduced to golf, I became a caddy. Not long after, the club where I caddied acquired half dozen of the first golf carts on the market. The caddies felt threatened and prepared to strike. However, it turned out these machines had been purchased for the halt and the lame, people whose physical capacity for golf had been lost, people who needed to ride to play. Indeed, those who wanted to use the carts had to produce a medical certificate testifying to their need. To the relief of the older men in the caddy yard who used the extra income for their families, the carts were quickly reserved every weekend by members we'd never seen before, and we all kept our old loops.

Yet the wall had been breached, an era had ended, and we had glimpsed the future: those middle-aged men and women who roared around us could have walked. They should have walked, being generally overweight and inactive. But golf carts are now accepted as part of the golfing experience. A generation of golfers has grown up using them, the caddies are gone, and courses now count on the carts for extra income.

Still, I wish Shivas Irons could have mysteriously appeared among us on that awful day. Large, graceful, scowling from under his Tam O'Shanter with fierce blue eyes, I would have him stride onto the fairways waving his mighty arms, throwing thunderbolts from his long fingers, and shouting, "The gemme is meant for walkin'!" That apparition would have cleared the course.

THE HAWTHORNE EFFECT

In psychology, there is a famous case study from the mid-1920's which demonstrated a principle that came to be known simply as "the Hawthorne effect". In the early days of industrial engineering, researchers working in the Hawthorne, Illinois, plant of Western Electric were looking for ways to increase productivity in an assembly area. In one experiment it was decided to dim the lights in the work space. Immediately, production increased. Then, after a time, production peaked and even declined to its original level. Discouraged researchers returned the plant illumination to normal and were pleasantly surprised to see another leap in productivity. But, again. production peaked then declined to its former level. Additional experiments produced similar results.

One obvious conclusion was that humans respond positively to change of any kind. Critics of the experiment suggested that when changes occurred employees felt they were being observed and would boost production until they felt "safe" again. In any event, the changes served to increase awareness of their performances among the involved individuals.

Isn't this what happens when the golfer changes clubs or some element of his grip, stance, or swing? Every one of us has had a few good rounds after changing a putter, driver, or wedge. Then, after losing awareness and the new "feel", our games return to their previous levels–the Hawthorne effect.

Should one then change clubs frequently? Perhaps we should change after a bad round. Perhaps after three bad rounds. Although we know "it isn't the clubs" as our spouses are bound to tell us, making the change is often all that is needed to awaken a sleeping game. The same thing goes for the swing tips we get from magazines and friends. The new "feel" serves to temporarily raise awareness and concentration.

"I've got it now" we shout in jubilation as we play a few good shots, good holes, even a few good rounds. Inevitably, we return to our former levels of play as the exotic grip or stance or club becomes ordinary.

Knowing this, one can always stay with the old reliable clubs and simply wait out the bad patch. Or put them away for a week or two—this also produces an improvement when we return to the game and is much cheaper!

I find I do best by committing to a putter/driver/wedge for a period of time. My overall *average* performance over the long run is what counts, not one hot round (although in an 18-hole tournament that could be the winner).

Whatever you do, don't sell the clubs you've set aside, or you won't have anything to change to when the new favorites lose their feel. Treat that putter or wedge or driver with the respect it's earned and give it a rest in a dark closet. The day will come when its magic will be restored for you. The Hawthorne effect is valid in golf; go ahead and use it to your advantage.

HIT THE BALL WITH YOUR BELLY

"The flatbellies can't play in Class AA," joked one of the better—and overweight—golfers in our county association. Indeed, several of the top players in the area are big men. Does girth improve performance? I've occasionally made some good swings and hit solid shots when I tried to "hit the ball with my belly," that is, make a good turn with the hips, away and through. It seems to help if you *imagine* you're fat!

Today, I got some confirmation from Joe Hyams' *Zen in the Martial Arts*, especially the chapter called "Extend your Ki." Apparently, *ki* is a powerful, but invisible life force (everyone has it—even a baby) which is centered about 1-1/2" below the navel.

This tremendous life force is "centered" about the natural center of gravity of the human body, and it is available to everyone through simple awareness.

"Think of the belly as a valve which sends water (*ki*) through all the extremities. When the valve is open, more water (energy) is generated through the legs and arms ... with your mind, you project this energy through your body in the direction you wish—you can be said to be extending your *ki*. *Ki* can be sent in any direction, depending on what you plan to do." (Hyams, p. 56)

One of the keys to unlocking this power for golfers seems to be that of "centering" the handle/shaft of the golf club. At address I check to see that the shaft is pointing directly at my naval or *ki* center. The relationship is maintained throughout the backswing and downswing. For example: when the club is horizontal to the ground on the back-swing, I can pause to check to make sure the club is still centered. Since my body has turned with the movement of the arms, it's usually perfect. As I practice swing, I can also check to see that the relationship is the same at impact and again at waist height as the club swings through toward the target. You'll be surprised how power-ful you feel when you achieve an awareness of the "centered" relationship. Famed teacher Jimmy Ballard calls this "triangle and center" in his "golf connection" concept. (Ballard, 79)

Golfers who set up so that the club shaft points outside of center—sometimes outside their bodies completely—will find it difficult or impos-sible to tap this power source. While many are apparently successful, using hand and arm strength to power the shot, they will usually be inconsistent. Their apparent success is based on pure talent and could have been even greater if they'd learned to hit the ball with their bellies and extend *ki* throughout the arc of the swing and, ultimately, the arc of the shot.

SOURCES

Ballard, Jim. *How to Perfect Your Golf Swing*. Golf Digest. Trumbull, CT: 1981.

Hyams, Joe. *Zen in the Martial Arts*. Bantam Books. New York: 1988

THE MOMENT OF TRUTH

Dan Millman, who offers a unique training in personal growth known as The Way of the Peaceful Warrior, speaks of seeking the "moment of truth" as we confront our fears. We recall the term from bull fighting, but seldom link it to other activities unless death is involved, as in hunting or war. But these, too, are games, suggests Millman. Though deadly serious, hunting and war are games in which man seeks to confront and discover himself. "The skill and courage and strength of the warrior are turned not against an external enemy, but against the inner enemies of egotism, fear, selfishness, and small mindedness." (Fields, 53)

In what we regard as a civilized arena, we daily test ourselves in games of school, business, and relationships. Yet, nowhere can the individual moment of truth be identified more clearly than in sport, particularly in individual sports such as golf. Where does your moment of truth appear? On the first tee? The final green? In the bunker? Where does fear rise in your heart like a hissing snake?

For me, it's the short putt. Just three feet from the cup is where I confront my fear, my ego, my self. Over the years I've panicked at these shots, stabbed and jabbed at the ball, trying to "wish" it into the hole, hurrying to get it over with, running from the snake which has become a raging bull!

Yet I find myself returning again and again to this confrontation. I recall trying to play in tournaments as a junior golfer, and into my twenties, and being in such a state of panic I could barely see the target, swing the club, or hit the ball. My swing must have been unrecognizable. I was so excited I'd slash at the ball wildly, blindly, hoping something good would happen. The predictable disasters occurred. I couldn't break 80; sometimes I couldn't break 90! I tore up cards, walked off the course, embarrassed myself, and aggravated others. I was an emotional wreck. Eventually, I gave up golf for several years.

Away from the game, I found peace of sorts; but the bull was always waiting for me. The Minotaur lived in the labyrinth of my being. Sometimes I'd hear him snorting in the mist, or just on the other side of a wall, close enough to touch.

"The way to get over fear is just to do it," Millman says. "You don't wait for it to go away. You act. That's the warrior's approach to life." (Fields, 57) But one can't act effectively out of a panicked state. One can only act effectively from a calm, peaceful state of mind. So, fear must be acknowledged and set aside, and the stroke or shot performed from a state of calm concentration, a kind of emptiness.

"Clear mirror, quiet water" is the state of mind the samurai warrior wanted to achieve. Not during peaceful meditation in a quiet garden, but in the heat of battle, at the point of a sword. This is the state of mind I need to cultivate to deal with my little moment of truth.

I'm doing better. Sometimes the old demons return, I panic, and the bull still gores me. But I'm getting better. Recently, I missed a short putt to double-bogey the first hole of an event. I was bleeding where both horns had pierced me. But I gathered myself, quieted my screaming, chattering, blue jay mind, and really got into the game. During the rest of the round I was tested 12 times. Twelve times I knocked those two-to-four-foot putts into the cup. I became totally focused. Concentrated on a single point. One with the ball, the club, the grass, and the cup.

I shot 82. Not a good score, but I felt victorious. As in the Zen art of archery, "the true target...is internal; the arrow is aimed at our egos, the seat of delusive thought. Whether or not one hits the external target—a piece of paper 90 feet away—is incidental. (Kushner, 59). What matters is the spirit with which one shoots." (Kushner, 56) Likewise, whether my golf ball drops into the cup or not—and some days it won't—is incidental. If I roll the ball simply and truly, from a clear heart and quiet mind, that is enough.

SOURCES

Fields, Rick. "Gentle Warrior." *Yoga Journal*, March/April 1989, pp. 52-57, 105, 107.

Kushner, Kenneth. "The Zen Art of the Bow." *Yoga Journal*, July/August 1989, pp. 54-59, 93.

PATIENCE

"Patience means restraining yourself. There are seven emotions... Joy, anger, anxiety, adoration, grief, fear, and hate. If a man doesn't give way to these, he's patient."

> *–Lord Toranaga*
> *Shogun by James Clavell*

My golf game has been undone by joy as well as anger. Two years ago, while playing in a local open, I unexpectedly birdied holes 6 and 7–and 7 was the toughest on the course! Totally elated, I swaggered to the eighth tee certain I was capable of winning the tournament. I quickly set the ball on the tee and–without so much as a practice swing topped it 50 yards into a begonia bush in the left rough!

Needless to say, I was shocked. What happened? I felt betrayed. I thought it was OK to play mindless golf. "Step up and hit it. You think too much," I'm often told. But this has happened more than once to many of us. We follow up birdies with bogeys or worse. (I made a double-bogey on that eighth hole, wiping out my birdies.)

One thing that goes on when we succumb to feeling joy (or any of the other emotions) is we abandon our pre-shot routine, thinking that—now we have mastered the game—we can dispense with such details! Without that ritual, we don't get properly set to the ball in the proven manner—and the shot is spoiled before we even waggle the club.

I firmly believe that our golf shots are made as we grip the club, address the ball, and assume our stance. Shots are made when we "feel" ready, calling up that sense of positive anticipation that comes from past success, perhaps on the driving range. Confidence is also built by monitoring one or two check points such as grip pressure and ball position.

These feelings are in the realm of awareness rather than conscious thought. But they cannot be skipped. ("*Patience means restraining yourself.*") We need to be patient enough to work through a proven routine every time.

To be patient doesn't mean we slow down play, going slower and slower as the value of the shot increases. Nor should one speed up as I did! Patience means we stick to our ritual, hitting the checkpoints we have proven work for us, time after time, shot after shot, right to the end, finishing the game.

Patience means never giving in to the emotions Lord Toranaga listed in the epigraph to this piece. I admit to experiencing joy after a good round–but I've learned that the score wouldn't have been so good if I'd started celebrating early. And I can never afford the other, more negative emotions, even after a round: they are simply too destructive, even physically debilitating.

Even joy is hollow and short-lived when one realizes that the wonderful score is probably the best one can do, and not a new average; and that a great round happens only a few times per season, especially in competition.

Yet, I do permit myself a small indulgence in joy once I am safely in the clubhouse with a satisfying number. Perhaps that is what we should really permit ourselves to experience– satisfaction–for I have been seduced and deceived by Joy.

THE SCORECARD CEREMONY

I've developed a new ritual to combat my constant anxiety over my golf score. I call it the scorecard ceremony. On the first tee, I simply take out a blank scorecard and tear it up. If the starter—or consideration for the ecology—would permit me, I'd throw the four sections high into the wind. The importance of this ceremony is its symbolism: One is saying, "I don't care about the score." This amounts to a conscious decision and will relieve a lot of pressure to perform well.

"Of course, you do," the ego whispers furtively. But you can refute that. You can take control of the day away from the ego and simply enjoy the game and the course and

your partners. You can consciously decide
that the score really doesn't matter.

You can also make a vow not to
renege on your decision once you're out on the
course. You'll need willpower—and practice—
to do this because tearing up the scorecard
really works. The problem is you sometimes
realize how well you're playing and suddenly
want your scorecard back! One way of
combating this impulse is to again "choose"
not to acknowledge your plus/minus status in
relation to par. Of course, the score has to be
recorded, especially in competition. But how
much better the results and our own
relaxation will be if we don't "peek."

What I'm suggesting is putting aside
all the mental arithmetic and calculations and
projections we perform, not only after com-
pleting a hole, but while we're standing in the
fairway, waiting to play a shot! If possible,
have a playing partner keep score for the
entire group, or concentrate on keeping your
partner's card accurate if you exchange them
as is so often the case in competition.

Tearing up the scorecard is a great
gift to your subconscious in that you've decided to enter the state of "no mind" and let your
body feel and play the game as well as it can—
and that will be very well indeed, probably

beyond your wildest expectations. It is also a great gift to your total being because getting free of the ego trap which demands perfection and criticizes our performances is a very liberating experience which will enhance your pleasure in the game of golf.

I currently collect old blank scorecards in my bag, not only to write on when we've forgotten to pick one up at the clubhouse, but to use in my scorecard ceremony. My wish is that all golfers would perform this little ritual on the first tee. It has great symbolic value and can set the tone for a wonderful day. I imagine if many people did it long enough, the ceremony would evolve to the point that the pro shop would have to set out little one-inch squares of paper so we could tear these up rather than the cards. At the very least, rend a corner of your game card with your fingernail. Do this quietly and deliberately and free yourself to really enjoy the game.

SEE IT DONE

Whenever I stand over a putt and can get a vivid, detailed mental picture of the ball rolling into the center of the cup, I almost always make it. Whenever I forget to do this or the picture isn't clear because I hurried, I'll usually miss. This kind of "one-pointed awareness" is the essence of concentration. One way I've found to enhance the frequency of, and quality of these mental pictures is to *see it done.*

"See" the ball in the bottom of the cup. "Hear" the sound as it falls in. "Watch" the label as it topples over the edge. (All this is a mental picture as you stand over the ball ready to stroke and looking at the cup.) Now, what did it take to put the ball there? Do that. Work backwards, so to speak, and make whatever stroke was necessary to complete the image. It will be the perfect stroke. But, first, "see it done."

Lately, I've been extending this technique to the full shots, "seeing" the ball resting perfectly on the green following its flight backward and down to the ball at my feet, then making the backswing and throughswing needed to strike the ball right back down this imaginary path to its resting place on the green. You won't even need to think about the swing; you'll *feel* exactly how to hit the ball to accomplish the imagined result.

On the longest shots we almost never establish a clear picture of the result. "Hit it toward the electric tower, on that next hill," we advise one another. "Aim for the chimney on the clubhouse" is another possibility. But that is only a directional target. We really don't want to—and probably couldn't—hit the ball over the clubhouse roof which is 500 or 600 yards away!

As with the shorter shots, "see it done" when addressing the tee ball and pick out a spot on the fairway where you want to see the ball at rest: a *distance* as well as directional target. I think we are reluctant to do this because we want to hit the ball as far as possible every time. Picking a fairway target may be limiting. But my experience has been that if I can get out to the 150-yard marker on every par four hole, I can *score*. In fact, I was astonished on my last two rounds when, with 150-yard posts in the rough beside the fairway, I began hitting my tee shot right to the base of the stake!

I quickly learned to switch to a brown or green spot on the fairway about the same distance out. Then, I followed the flight back to the ball and made the swing I needed to put it there. It's surprising how often you can drop the ball right on the spot you picked, even when you slightly mis-hit it.

"See it done" and you'll know exactly what to do. "See it done" and DO IT!

SELF TALK

The power of the subconscious mind to accept and act upon suggestions has been well-documented but was demonstrated very vividly to me a few years ago. Upon returning from summer vacation to the college where I teach, I found it difficult to get back to work. One day, not long after the start of the fall semester, I was walking down a sunny corridor, looking at the beautiful autumn day through the window, saying to myself, "I can't stand this. I've got to get out of here." I said these words silently, but intensely.

Within two hours, I had collapsed in my office. As I watched the building recede between my feet from inside the ambulance, I clearly heard my subconscious mind say something like, "OK. We're out of here. What's next?"

I recovered fairly quickly that afternoon. Doctors could find nothing wrong, and I returned to work the next day. But I now had an operational definition of the activity of the subconscious mind. We all have made ourselves ill from time to time. Some people make themselves seriously ill; indeed, some researchers claim that all ailments have psychosomatic roots. Medicine is just discovering that we also have the power to make ourselves well, and that many times we can accomplish this—without the aid of drugs—through a variety of processes such as imaging and meditation.

It is the subconscious which the hypnotist addresses because it is so open to suggestions. It is also absolutely literal, being unable to recognize the subtleties of humor or sarcasm. When I asked to be checked out of my work that day, the subconscious—which controls our automatic, physical being—obliged in the only manner it could. I have since learned to monitor my self-talk, and to change negative statements into positive ones.

The following statements are direct quotes overheard on or near the golf course:

"I never chip in. I haven't holed a chip shot in years!"

"I can't buy a short putt."

"I have a terrible slice."

"I'll never be any good."

Of course, the subconscious mind—one of the most powerful forces in our being—hears these statements and takes steps to make them come true. Is it any surprise that our troubles continue? While one cannot deny reality—changes in technique and adequate practice may be necessary to correct some of these problems—real improvement probably will not come about so long as we continue making negative suggestions to ourselves.

What could be said in the above cases?

"I'm due to chip the ball into the hole. Maybe I'll make this one."

"I make most of my short putts, and there's no reason why I shouldn't make this one. I'll roll it into the cup."

"I'm going to set aside my fear of slicing and let my arms swing through to hit a straight ball or even a hook!"

"When I think about my first attempts to play golf, I realize how much I've improved."

Such positive statements are called "affirmations", and all of us need to develop them for use on the course—and throughout life—so our self-talk becomes a positive force rather than a destructive one. The steps are simple:

1. *Monitor the inner (and sometimes oral) statements we make about ourselves and our performance.*

2. *Convert the statement into an affirmation.*

It is particularly powerful to write these down. Speak them aloud when discussing play with friends. The sub-conscious will respond quickly when such statements appear outside the body to be read through the eyes or heard through the ears.

Becoming aware of our self-talk through the monitoring process will help us to uncover how negative our attitudes often are. How often we verbally abuse ourselves after missing a putt or dubbing a shot, saying "You idiot!" "Dummy!" Surely, we deserve better treatment from ourselves. In 1988, professional Scott Verplank made a vow to simply smile after every shot, no matter what the result. Scott went on to win the Buick Open and $366,045. Replacing those negative judgments and instructions with positive affirmations will help us to succeed in golf and the other games of life.

SINCERITY

Sincerity, n.   not feigned or affected; true. 2. presenting no false appearance; honest, clean, pure, genuine.

What the world is suffering most from is a lack of sincerity. It is the age of comedian Don Rickles in which we trade insults rather than compliments. Seldom is a message framed sincerely and delivered directly. Indeed, the language and tones of sincerity have been misused so often by the equivalent of vice-presidents, salesmen, and televangelists that they are immediately distrusted.

Thus, sincerity is an attitude (as is the absence of sincerity) which profoundly influences the way we behave toward each other and ourselves. In his book, *The Inner Game of Golf*, Tim Gallwey describes an encounter with a Buddhist monk whose brothers work at maintaining the golf course he is playing. Gallwey is advised to play—indeed, live—with "utmost sincerity."

"The phrase struck a deep chord in me," said Gallwey. "Utmost sincerity is what's left when you stop trying to be anything, when there are no more expectations or pictures to live up to." (Gallwey, 160)

People fake sincerity. They look into your eyes and lie. Sometimes we play along with the game, especially in business or at work, often in relationships until the weight of the dishonesty destroys them. Sometimes we even lie to ourselves, convincing ourselves that something is true when it isn't, just because we want it to be.

We tell tall stories about our golf scores, imagining our desired successes to be real, when in truth were we to play the game correctly—sincerely—our scores would be several strokes higher. Answer truly, whether you follow these few basic tenets of golf:

1) Play the ball as it lies.

2) Play the course as you find it.

3) Hole out all putts.

We hedge on the first one a great deal. I, too, like the USGA "winter rules" which permit us—usually in one's own fairway—to lift, clean, and place the ball in a preferred lie within one club length of its original location, but not nearer the hole. (Rules, 91) If we must have preferred lies, I'd rather do this than bat the ball around with the clubhead, as so many do. (Besides, it's nice to be able to clean the ball.) However, my overall experience is that *I hit better shots and score lower when I don't touch the ball at all.* Even though I know this to be true, in a tournament which permits preferred lies I find myself going along with the corruption, lest I find myself at a disadvantage. Somehow, I lack sincerity.

We *usually* play the course as we find it, if we can resist the temptation to break off or bend tree branches in our way—or even not pull up the dandelion stems behind the ball, in order to have an unobstructed swing. This is not sincerity.

"That's good. Inside the leather," we say to one another on the putting green. Without even measuring. (Measuring here means to lay the putter on the green with its toe in the cup. If the ball is no farther out than the bottom of the grip on the shaft, many foursomes concede these putts. Obviously, this can only be done in head-to-head match play as the rest of the field in a tournament may not be as generous.) A notoriously poor short putter, I find myself unwilling to concede anything. The ball goes in the cup, period. And we count *every* stroke it takes to put it there.

Play the ball as it lies. Play the course as you find it. Hole out all putts. That's sincerity.

SOURCES

The Rules of Golf. United States Golf Association. Far Hills, NJ: 1991.

Gallwey, Timothy W. *The Inner Game of Golf,* Random House, New York: 1981.

Rules of Golf. United States Golf Association. Far Hills, NJ: 1991.

THE STRANGER

It's happened three times this season, and I now understand there is a purpose and a message in it. During the week, I like to get out on the golf course alone, to be with my thoughts, to practice, to simply play without the distraction of socializing with others. I also like to play two balls, thus playing 18 holes, while only walking—and paying for—nine.

Inevitably, I'll look back from a green or tee and see a lone golfer hurrying to catch up. I usually cringe. Since I'm playing two balls, I can be caught. Sometimes I eliminate the practice swing, walk faster, stop aligning putts. But, always, the stranger overtakes me. This time, a short, sturdy man in his mid-30's came waddling toward the green where I'd just marked the two balls, I hit out of the bunker on the first hole. He was wearing camouflage hunting pants, a blue t-shirt, and a black baseball cap. He was pulling a bag racked on a rented pull-cart which had a medium-sized cooler hanging from its handle. He didn't seem to be playing a ball. Maybe he was headed for the second tee.

"Please go ahead and play through," I called over to him. He stopped beside the green, pulled out a can of beer from the cooler, and grinned at me as he popped the top.

"I was hoping we could play together," he said. I hesitated, feeling irritated over this invasion of my privacy. It was getting to be too familiar. "I'm playing two balls," I explained. "It's my own little game."

"That's OK," the stranger said, smiling even more broadly. "I just like to have somebody to go around with."

"Damn," I muttered, picking up my markers. As usual, I was torn between my selfish needs and practicing the most common courtesy on the course.

"Well, you'll have to wait until I hit from the blue tee," I growled as we walked over to number two. I was still trying to discourage him. I teed up and hit two three-wood shots to the opening of the right-hand dogleg. There was water on the right side of the hole. These were perfect shots.

I turned to my bag while he teed up his ball, determined not to watch. I heard the swoosh and click as his ball was struck. Again, my new partner turned to me, smiling and talking slowly. I wondered if he were already intoxicated.

"Well, I guess I won't be going around with you after all. That was my only golf ball."

"Did you hit it in the river?" I asked incredulously.

"Yep. Right off the toe. I'll have to go in now." He stood there, waiting expectantly, knowing what I'd say.

"Here," I said, feigning politeness. I tossed him an old ball from my bag. He beamed like a child at Christmas.

"Thanks!" The next shot was sliced, too, but stayed in play. Away we went, then, down the fairway. Angry, I walked faster and faster, but the stranger had no trouble keeping up. When we reached the balls, it turned out he'd outdriven me. I grabbed a four-iron and made two, quick, smooth swings, rocketing the balls greenward. One was pin-high to the left. The other was on line but fell short.

"Nice shot, Joe," my companion said with such genuine enthusiasm I felt guilty. He punched his shot (my ball) up close to the green, and we walked on in silence.

The stranger demonstrated a soft touch around the greens, chipping up close and rolling in the short putt. I bogeyed the hole with both balls, missing short putts for pars. It went this way for the next few holes, although I had to "loan" him three more balls. He offered to pay a dollar for the third one, but I refused. "They're old balls," I insisted.

After hitting a tee shot into the lake on the fifth, I gave up playing two balls. I was rattled, having three-putted the previous green. Now I was confused as well as angry. Giving up helped. It always helps to surrender to the golf course. As soon as I stop trying, I begin playing better; however, this usually happens too late in the round to save the score. I also began feeling more sympathy—and less resentment—toward my playing partner.

Still, I was disappointed over being forced to play with someone again. I vowed to simply, flatly refuse the next time.

"I'm going home to train my two beagle pups." the stranger said as I chipped close for a par on the final hole. In fact, I'd parred the final four holes, and the last two were the toughest on the course!

Come to think of it, the stranger had parred them, too, despite his slashing swing. At least it was over. My game was intact, maybe even better than usual. I began to feel guilty again over my lack of warmth toward a fellow linksman. I could afford to be nice now. It wouldn't cost a thing.

In the parking lot, we both went to the pickup trucks we'd arrived in. Mine was a new, white Jeep. His was rusty, old red Chevy which smoked a lot when he started it. The stranger leaned out the window and grinned as he passed the spot where I was sitting on the tailgate, changing shoes. "Bye, Joe," he said warmly. I smiled back and waved like a gracious competitor.

Then his truck was gone, the bald tires crunching on the gravel, threatening to puncture on the sharp stones and broken tile from the clay plant across the road.

Was it Christ? The Buddha? And why do these avatars continue to visit me in disguise? Part of this stiffness in attitude causes the stiffness in my swing. (I was appalled to discover on videotape that I'd already acquired a "senior" swing. It was especially disheartening to compare this with an old 8mm film taken 30 years ago when I was twenty and had a full, free-swinging action.)

And so, he comes, following me, pursuing me when I am alone until I understand: he is my missing part, the part which enjoys life, relaxes, is social and warm. He is all that I am not, but need to become: carefree, loving, comfortable and at ease in the world, content with his golf game which he laughs at, knowing it is meaningless.

The next time I see my other self following me, I hope I will recognize him. In his frustration at not being able to join with me, his outer form constantly changes, hoping I will accept him. Indeed, I shall embrace him when I can find the courage to become a truly integrated golfer and person.

SURRENDER

I sometimes deal poorly with the usual adversities one encounters during a round of golf. Fear—of failure or success, it doesn't matter—has particularly affected my performance, resulting in an even more devastating emotion: anger. The negative self-talk which follows (... you stupid *+%# .... how can you be so dumb .... etc.) completes the cycle until the score for the day is ruined.

Amazingly, at this point, when it is no longer possible to reach my scoring goal for the day, when I am emotionally exhausted from beating myself up, after I completely, totally surrender—my game blossoms, and I'm able to play the second nine or final few holes somewhere close to par.

This phenomenon repeated itself often enough to reveal a pattern: *I could only score when I didn't try.* Somehow, after all is lost, I stop trying, let my swing become natural and free, and hit the ball without even thinking—to score par after par!

A variation of this pattern occurs when one is able to hold things together for most of the round, working patiently through adversity, to find oneself on the 15th tee just four over par for the day. Par in for 76. The last time this happened to me, I played the next three holes bogey, double-bogey, par—so I then stood at 18 tee needing a par to break 80. Oh, how often I've done this to myself! Bogey—80.

Perhaps the fear of success is at work here. What if I begin to play regularly in the 70's? What if I have a chance to win a tournament? What would I have left to complain about or work on?

Whatever the source of the fear, it feels the same; and the problem of trying emerges. Standing on the 15th tee, our self-talk subtly changes. Instead of playing the course one shot at a time, heedless of score, as we had been doing, we become careful, trying for specific scores on each hole. In doing this, *we stop the event from naturally unfolding*!

It doesn't matter whether we become conservative or aggressive. (I've got to birdie in to break 75.) We begin to try, which—in golf and other activities in life—frequently leads to failure.

Of course, this is not supposed to be happening, we reason. Having been taught almost from birth to never give up, and "if at first you don't succeed, try, try again," we enter a state of psychological shock since—as we try ever harder—we perform even worse!

Without trying to make a particular score, concentrate on one swing thought, a *feel* actually, which is a key for you. (For me, it's feeling my back square to the target at the top of the swing.) "Let" the shot happen as a result. Walk down the fairway to the ball. Do it again. And again. Discipline yourself to continue playing one shot at a time until you walk off the 18th green.

Surrender to your fate. (It won't be nearly as bad as you imagine.) Don't anticipate bad things—or even good things. Just Play. Swing. Hit. Count the strokes when it's over. Much like painting or calligraphy, each stroke is unique and can never be replayed. Appreciate it. Sometimes even poor strokes set us up for a compensating good shot. Let the round happen to you, rather than trying to cause something to happen.

Our scores are our scores, much like our signatures for the day or the canvas that we painted upon. "In the Oriental calligraphic tradition ... every brush stroke must be decisive, with no going back. It's just like the things we do in life." (K. Tanahashi)

Each round of golf has its own uniqueness if we'll have the patience to let it develop fully. Accept the score as an honest and complete expression of what you are, here and now. Whatever that is, is OK.

The beautiful thing about this approach is that fear has vanished from consideration as we explore what the round will become. And let it be.

SWING THE CLUBHEAD

The spirit of Ernest Jones visited me last night. It was at a point of abysmal despair that the kindness appeared at 2 or 3 a.m. I'd lost my swing–and game–during the previous week's World Amateur Championship at Myrtle Beach. Carl Lohren's "one move to better golf" wasn't working, and I was struggling to break 90 at this week's tournament. (This day's round: 45-46-91)

Jones appeared standing, then sitting near my motel room bed. There was a luminous glow around him, and while he certainly wasn't youthful, he looked in ruddy good health. His hair was thin and sandy, and he was wearing glasses, although I don't recall many pictures of Jones with glasses. He was wearing a dark blue suit. white shirt, and red bow tie. (I later realized I may have been confusing Jones' image with that of his son-in-law and assistant, Fred Austin, who appeared in *Golf Illustrated* recently with what may be the final word on Jones' simple swing theory.)

Anyway, the ghost of the grand, old professional spoke clearly to me. "Use those wonderful hands," he said indulgently, folding mine together inside his warm, soft hands. "Swing the club with the hands," he remonstrated. And I realized he was right: Lohren's method ignores the hands, trusting them to work "instinctively." "That takes away your most valuable asset," Jones insisted in his clipped, British accent, apparently reading my thoughts. Were we communicating telepathically, as sometimes happens in dreams?

"Stop worrying about turning and twisting individual parts of your body while trying to hold other things still," he went on. "Swing the clubhead!" he thundered.

Again, I knew he was right. I'd completely lost my swing and my confidence as I tried to grip the club tighter and tighter with a stronger and stronger left-hand grip. The quality of my shots was deteriorating into those weak little short-right hits, and I was gripping tighter, swinging harder, and mis-hitting more and more.

By the end of the previous day, it was evident that all my rhythm and timing was gone. I was trying to force the ball into the air using what Jones has condemned as "leverage." Like the alcoholic, I'd hit bottom, visited the pits. My game was at its nadir, the lowest point in years.

"Stop trying to do anything," Jones continued, putting his arm around me as we sat side by side on the edge of the bed. "Stand relaxed to the ball with your hips, shoulders, and feet in line with the target. Then swing the club back and through as if it were a weight on a string. You know how to do it. Relax and feel the freedom of true swinging!"

What about the score? I wanted to know. The answer was obvious. Good swinging will lead to good scoring. Swing the driver. Swing the putter and the wedges and the middle irons. Stop trying to lever the ball around the course.

Can I break 90 today? Of course, Jones assured me. Will you come with me today? He merely nodded. (Indeed, he did appear beside the sixth green as I was waiting to putt a short one. I felt especially good as I'd hit the biggest drive of the day, right

down the middle of the fariway. He smiled
benevolently, then slowly faded into the
sunlight. I was called to putt by my playing
partners, and when I looked again, Jones had
disappeared.)

I went on to shoot 45-44-89, and felt a
little better about my game. The course we
were playing was tough, and I was just
returning to swinging. Later that night, the
spirit of Ernest Jones visited me again. Both
my knees had been aching all summer, and I'd
hurt my back in July. I'd been wrapping the
knees alternately, not wanting to have both
bandaged at the same time! Jones merely
watched me unwrap and undress.

"You're the man to talk with about
bad legs, aren't you?" I said. Instantly, I
regretted the intimacy. But it seemed natural
to discuss it. Jones had lost his lower right leg
in WWI, then shot an 81 while standing on
one leg in his first round back! (Later, he
would play par golf with an artificial limb—
and this was long before the appearance of
golf carts.)

He smiled and said, "Got a couple of
bad knees, have you? And a sore back? It's
no wonder you're hurting as you're using
leverage to move the ball, not a swing." Jones
doesn't want me to swing hard. But *fast*.

Swing the clubhead! is based not so much on strength but speed. He reminded me again of that Newtonian statement from physics: Force = Mass x Acceleration ...

At that point I must have either awakened or fallen out of the dream. But I recall the event clearly. This was one of those apparitions one sees in his darkest hours. Truly, "when the student is ready, the teacher will appear."

The following morning, I awoke feeling very rested, light, and refreshed. I hit the first ball 240 yards with such an easy swing it was frightening. Then I staked iron shots on the first three holes. While I didn't make any birdie putts, they were easy, easy pars, and I knew. I just knew.

WHAT IS ZEN?

"What is Zen?" I am frequently asked as I talk to groups of golfers about the spiritual and psychological aspects of the game. I want to reply that "Zen is nothing, yet everything." But I fear losing the students' attention. Sometimes I explain that the Japanese word *Zen* comes from the Chinese *ch'an*. The original Sanskrit word is *dhyana*. (Watts, 54) It is interesting that this sequence of translations tracks the thousand-year journey of Buddhism from India to China and Japan.

"But what does it mean?" A number of scholars have offered definitions. Dictionaries and encyclopedias treat the word as a label identifying a Buddhist sect. Alan Watts has said "dhyana ... can best be described as

the state of unified or one-pointed awareness."
(Watts, 55)

In his book, *An Introduction to Zen Buddhism*, the eminent scholar D.T. Suzuki names an entire chapter "What is Zen?" then spends ten pages *not* answering the question. Indeed, Suzuki leaves us with the insistence that Zen is as mysterious as it is mystical because it is so fundamentally simple it cannot be discussed in language.

"An ancient master, wishing to show what Zen is, lifted one of his fingers, another kicked a ball, and a third slapped the face of his questioner ... is not Zen the most practical and direct method of spiritual training ever resorted to by any religion?" (Suzuki, 45)

"One-pointed awareness."

Spontaneous action.

Do these not describe the "concentration" we seek in golf but seldom achieve? To the Western mind, concentration means trying hard, usually to achieve some result or objective. But the Zen archer focuses not on the result but the process of drawing his bow and shooting. He is aware of the target only because it is part of the process, not something to be knocked down or beaten.

"Put the thought of hitting (the target) right out of your mind," cries Eugen Herrigel's Japanese archery teacher in *Zen in the Art of Archery*. "You can be a master even if every shot does not hit. The hits on the target are only the outward proof and confirmation of your purposelessness at its highest, of your egolessness, your self-abandonment, or whatever you like to call this state." (Herrigel, 56)

All this suggests that we take a new look at our motives for playing golf, along with the processes we use. It is evident that the archery master would have us "concentrate" on the swing rather than the score. It is also evident that, to succeed in any psycho-physical activity (archery, bowl-ing, golf, fencing, etc.) we need to abandon the ego, the self which is so concerned with results. Earlier in Herrigel's book the master tells him:

"The more obstinately you try to learn how to shoot the arrow for the sake of hitting the goal, the less you will succeed ... What stands in your way is that you have a much too willful will." (p. 31)

It is at once most difficult (yet utterly simple) to let go of the will, the self, the ego, especially in a game such as golf where we are ultimately judged, compared, even grouped and rewarded by our scores. Thus, even our occasional victory is short-lived. We can go out the next day or week after winning a tournament and play our worst game. Then all the anger and frustration come flooding back, bringing the dragon of unhappiness with them. After a time, any human will grow weary of riding the undulating back of this monster.

Our salvation is to become pur-poseless and egoless in our play. And "play" is the right word. A child playing does not consider whether it is doing "good" or "bad", "right" or "wrong" in its simple games. The child simply experiences and enjoys the present moment with no awareness of the "self". It is the ego which makes judgments and sets the standards for our ultimate failures. But in forgetting ourselves, purpose-lessness and egolessness combine to become a spiritual state; a door opens for the sur-rendered self; and we become enlightened. Suddenly, there is no past, no future, only the present world in which we are perfectly at ease. There we can do no wrong. We experience a positive "flow" state (trance) and the score we once hoped for manifests itself almost independent of our actions.

Once, after a dramatic demonstration of his shooting skills, Herrigel's archery master declared "...it is not 'I' who must be given credit for this shot. 'It' shot and 'It' made the hit. Let us bow to the goal as before the Buddha." (Herrigel, 59)

Do you see that sport can be a passage to the spiritual life? I think many of us sense this—though we would be reluctant to discuss it among our weekend foursomes—and that the bond we feel with our playing companions is really a common striving to achieve transcendence through sport.

SOURCES

Herrigel, Eugen. *Zen in the Art of Archery* (Vintage Books 1989 edition) Random House: New York 1981.

Suzuki, Daisetz Teitaro. *An Introduction to Zen Buddhism.* Grove Press: New York 1964.

Watts, Alan W. *The Way of Zen.* Pantheon Books: New York 1957.

A GOLF PRAYER

Let nothing disturb my inner peace and joy today—not the turmoil of the first tee, nor chattering playing partners (and opponents) nor golfers waiting impatiently behind me, nor the pace of play.

Let me experience the expanse of the open sky and the golfing grounds and enjoy their variety in all the weathers. Let me smell the damp earth, feel the wind on my face, and hear the babbling brook beside the fairway while waiting for others to play.

Let me "trust and release", swinging the clubhead and feeling the power and flow of a spontaneous, natural swing. Let no thought intrude to tighten my muscles and spoil my shot. Let me swing freely (the putter, too) from a state of "no mind."

Let me play one shot at a time, as if each were the entire game. As the Zen archer says: "One shot, one life." And let me smile no matter what the result, for I am fortunate indeed to be here, enjoying free time in a free land.

And let me forget the score and the match and play the course itself, for it doesn't matter whether I score well or win; what matters is the spirit in which I play.

–JM

SUGGESTED READINGS

Dass, Ram. *Journey of Awakening; A Meditator's Guidebook.* Bantam Books, New York: 1990.

Ram Dass (Richard Alpert) is an American psychologist and spiritual teacher and experimenter. This book discusses the flow state and offers a variety of methods to achieve it through meditation practice.

Csikzentmihalyi, Mihalyi. *Flow; The Psychology of Optimal Experience.* Harper & Row, New York: 1990.

Csikzentmihalyi has made a lifelong study of the "flow" experience. This book condenses decades of research into a format for the general reader.

Enhager, Kjell. *Quantum Golf.* New York: 1991.

Enhager describes a "quantum" experience in learning golf through the format of the short novel. Each chapter concludes with exercises for the reader.

Gallwey, W. Timothy. *The Inner Game of Golf.* Random House, New York: 1981.

Gallwey's classic book on tennis was so successful he applied the principles to golf. Gallwey's "inner game" attempts to resolve the conflict between what he calls "self 1" and "self 2", which represent our conscious and sub-conscious minds. The book contains many narrative experiences of his own attempts to achieve relaxed concentration and play golf successfully.

Gawain, Shakti. *Creative Visualization.* Bantam Books, New York: 1979.

This easy to read and use workbook helps the reader to focus mental energy to transform health, attitude, and performance. Especially powerful are the exercises in positive affirmations and goal setting.

Hanh, Thich Nhat. *Peace is Every Step.* Bantam Books, New York: 1991.

Hanh, a Zen Buddhist monk from Vietnam, offers a simple, insightful method for achieving "mindfulness" and inner peace.

Herrigel, Eugen. *Zen in the Art of Archery.* Random House, New York: 1981.

As a German professor who taught philosophy at Tokyo University between the Wars, Herrigel sought to explore the mystery of Zen archery with a fiery master. Many of the concepts reported in this little classic can be directly applied to golf.

Hyams, Joe. *Zen in the Martial Arts.* Bantam Books, New York: 1988.

Hyams, a journalist and writer based in Hollywood, spent many years studying the martial arts and worked with Bruce Lee. He discusses Zen, flow states, and directed energy in the martial arts.

Millman, Dan. *The Warrior Athlete; Body, Mind & Spirit*. Stillpoint Publishing, Walpole, NH: 1979.

To become a champion gymnast, Millman struggled to integrate the classic trinity of body, mind, and emotions. This book represents his practical advice for training. Golf is mentioned often.

Millman, Dan. *Way of the Peaceful Warrior*. H.H. Kramer, Inc., Tiburon, CA: 1984.

In this novel, Miliman's hero interacts with Socrates, a shamanistic "warrior" who seems to have achieved enlightenment. Here, Millman presents the concept of being a "peaceful warrior" as opposed to our traditional concepts of primitive violence.

Murphy, Michael. *Golf in the Kingdom*. Dell Publishing, New York: 1972.

Murphy's now classic tale centers around the Scottish professional Shivas Irons whose mystical approach to golf seems to contain the keys to unlock the doors to our best games.

Suzuki, D.T. *An Introduction to Zen Buddhism*. Grove Press, New York: 1964.

As a professor of Buddhist philosophy, Dr. Suzuki has committed his life to explaining the philosophy and concepts of Zen to the Western reader. This required introduction to the subject, with a Foreword by C.G. Jung, was first published in 1954.

Trungpa, Chogyam. *The Sacred Path of the Warrior*. Bantam Books, New York: 1984.

Born in Tibet, Trungpa presents the principles and practices of an enlightened warrior culture. He maintains that the practice of "warriorship" against self-doubt, negativity, and aggression will lead us to personal happiness and fulfillment.

Watts, Alan W. *The Way of Zen*. Pantheon Books, New York: 1957.

Watts explores the background and history, then the principles and practices of Zen for western readers.

JOSEPH McLAUGHLIN

Joe is author of several books including the novella, *Golf is the Devil's Game*, which dramatizes the concepts of *Zen in the Art of Golf*. As a published author, his poems, short stories, reviews, essays, travel articles, and photographs have appeared in well over 100 publications, many of which are nationally distributed.

Early in life, McLaughlin was a caddy and an assistant golf professional. As a reinstated amateur (USGA) one of his greatest joys was developing and teaching a continuing education course called "Enjoy Golf!" The class was designed to introduce beginning players to the game. Over 150 men, women, and children learned the joy of golf through his instruction.

He and his wife Darlene played over 100 rounds each year. On Sunday mornings, they were joined by their children and spouses for many memorable rounds at "The Church on the Green."